My Fabulous Fashion Sketchbook

WENDY WARD & ROBYN NEILD

sourcebooks
jabberwocky

This book was conceived, designed & produced by

Ivy Press

CREATIVE DIRECTOR	Peter Bridgewater
MANAGING EDITOR	Hazel Songhurst
COMMISSIONING EDITOR	Georgia Amson-Bradshaw
ART DIRECTOR	Kim Hankinson
PROJECT EDITOR	Judith Chamberlain-Webber
DESIGNER	Lisa McCormick
ILLUSTRATORS	Robyn Neild &
	John Woodcock

Origination by Ivy Press Reprographics

Printed and bound in China

10 9 8 7 6 5 4 3 2 1

Parents, guardians, or care-givers are encouraged to actively
participate with their children when using the Internet or other electronic
resources, and to provide guidance for their usage.

Contents

Introduction

Do you love fashion and clothes? Would you like to know what fashion design is all about?

WHAT IS FASHION?

Fashion reflects our identities and our personalities, and fashion trends influence us in all kinds of ways. You can tell a lot about people from the clothes they wear: their age, their taste in music, their interests, and even how successful they are.

WHAT IS FASHION DESIGN?

From the outside, fashion design looks like a world of glamour and excitement. It can be all of these things, and is a highly creative industry. Think about this—all clothes, from designer dresses to what you are wearing right now, were ideas brought to life by a fashion designer.

BE A FASHION DESIGNER!

This book will show you how to design a fashion collection of your own. It will guide you through the design process from first ideas to final presentation. You can use the blank pages at the end of each section to collect ideas, create mood boards, sketch designs, play around with colors and shapes, and—finally—to present your collection.

Ideas

All design begins with an idea.
Pulling all your ideas together can seem
a little daunting at first. Where do you begin?
Where do you get your ideas?

This section will show you where
to start looking for ideas and what to do
with them once you have them.

Find ideas

LOOK FOR INSPIRATION...

Nope, not under your bed! But design ideas are everywhere. Here are a few suggestions to get you started.

Nature

Markets

Art &
museums

Fashion
shows

Different cultures

Fashions from
the past

Collect ideas

SAVE IMAGES YOU LIKE...

These might be drawings, fashion images from magazines, or clothes you have seen on the Internet.

TAKE PHOTOS

On his fashion blog "The Sartorialist," Scott Schuman posts "straight-ups" of ordinary people on the street. A "straight-up" is a full length photo of a person in everyday surroundings. Take some of your friends!

DESIGNER'S TIP

Save and record your ideas as sketches, samples, cut-outs, or photos in the scrapbook pages at the end of this section.

FABRIC SAMPLES

You can cut up your old clothes, look for fabrics and clothes in thrift shops, and ask friends and family for any unwanted clothing.

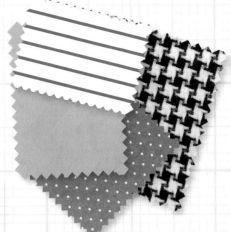

MAKE NOTES

Write down or draw your ideas in the sketchbook pages in this book (see the Designer's Tip opposite). Keep all your pictures together; even if you don't use them right away, they may be useful another time.

GO ONLINE

Pinterest and similar websites where people can post their creative ideas offer an easy way to collect ideas online and put them into themed "boards."

Create mood boards

Ideas are no good kept hidden in a folder or sketchbook. Fashion designers pull out the ones they like best and create mood boards.

Mood boards are like those little bulletin boards where you display all your favorite things. The ideas on a fashion mood board tell a story—this one is about Paris.

3546 — PARIS. La Tour Eiffel
et le Palais du Trocadéro.

RÉPUBLIQUE FRANÇAISE

CITY OF PARIS

DESIGNER'S BRIEF

Pick out some of your favorite pictures that have a similar theme. Use the scrapbook pages to make a mood board with a story and give it a title.

Jean-Charles de Castelbajac

METRO

Je t'aime Paris!

Marrakesh mood board

Shiny metallics, warm golds and oranges, and brilliant blues repeat in different images on this mood board. Using these colors in your palette would give a hot, summery, Moroccan feel to your design.

Gatsby mood board

There is so much pattern on this mood board! The very detailed repeating patterns and the shimmering gold tones give a rich, luxurious feel which you could use in your designs.

Summer blues

The range of blues on this minimal mood board would give your designs a fresh, outdoorsy feel.

Delicate white and strong blues!

Love the colors of blue in the sea

ONLINE

Online pin boards are a quick way to pull images together, and an easy way to remember where the pictures came from.

Using your mood boards

Now that you have collected your ideas into themed mood boards, look more carefully at the pictures. Make notes on the ones you like the best and pin them to the images.

Prom Night Inspiration

The pastel colors in the jewelry match the fabric

Diamanté touches to add sparkle

Pretty, fresh palette!

Marrakesh

Warm, glowing palette

Exotic colors and patterns

Beautiful embroidered detailing

DESIGNER'S BRIEF

Pull out your three favorite items from your mood board and write down what you like best about them.

Intricate linked pattern

Concept to catwalk

Here are some real-life examples of how ideas on a mood board can eventually turn into catwalk garments:

YVES SAINT LAURENT

is a French fashion designer who designed this dress in 1965 after being inspired by the geometric paintings of artist Piet Mondrian.

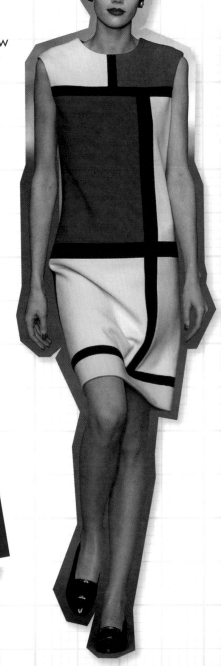

GUCCI,

an Italian design company, was influenced by traditional Russian costumes in the fine embroidery and detail in this collection.

VIVIENNE WESTWOOD

is famous for her quirky style. She is known for corseted, draped, luxurious dresses, and many pieces from this collection looked like walking oil paintings.

Catwalk to mall

Designer clothes are expensive! After designs have been shown on the catwalk, fashion retailers then quickly make their own versions that are more affordable and practical.

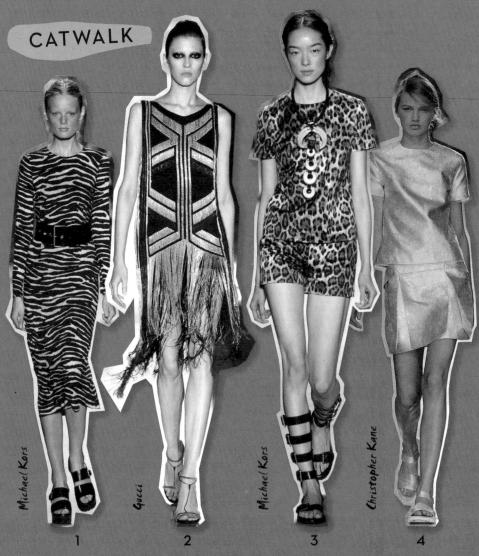

CATWALK

Michael Kors

Gucci

Michael Kors

Christopher Kane

1

2

3

4

FASHION STORES

A

B

C

D

DESIGNER'S BRIEF

Link the fashion store clothes to the catwalk designs that might have originally inspired them.

Predicting fashions

Fashion designers often work more than a year ahead, so how do they keep their ideas "on trend" and know what people will want to wear?

WHAT THEY DO

- Travel to other cities and countries
- Visit art exhibitions
- Research upcoming global events
- Watch movies and go to the theater
- Listen to the latest music
- Look at what people are wearing
- Listen to what people are talking about and what they're into

TREND COMPANIES

There are also trend forecasting companies that help designers know what will be the "must-have" item and what will be on trend. They can predict the colors, prints, fabrics, and silhouettes that will define the coming fashion seasons.

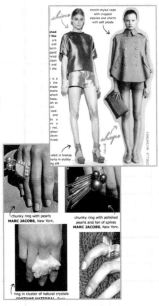

DESIGNER'S BRIEF

Identify three different trends among your friends. Take some "straight-up" photos (see page 10) to record them.

BLOGS

Some bloggers present their own smaller collections online, and sites such as Pinterest, Instagram, and Twitter are great ways to see what trends people are looking at right now.

Scrapbook pages for your ideas

Use these pages to create a scrapbook of your ideas. Do some drawing, take some photographs, begin a story, and see where it takes you!

Why not start by recording the things that represent YOU—your favorite music, colors, sport, hobbies, and so on?

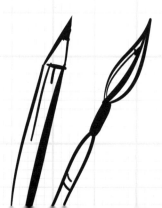

DESIGNER'S TIP

Do you have enough images to make
a mood board yet? You need about ten...
Don't forget to give your mood board
a title—remember it's telling a story.

DESIGNER'S TIP

If you have enough images for
more than one mood board, make
several—remember to give each
one a different story.

IDEAS SCRAPBOOK

Designing

OK, now that you have collected and organized your ideas, you can use them to start designing.

In this section, we'll look at colors, patterns, silhouettes, and how to draw clothes the "fashion" way.

Color

Color is an important part of fashion. The colors used in a collection are usually the first sign of the season, and each season will have its own "must-have" color.

USING A COLOR WHEEL

The primary colors are red, blue, and yellow. They're strong, bold colors that can't be created by mixing other colors.

Complementary colors are opposite on the color wheel. Placing two side by side makes both colors look brighter, so they are good for bold contrast.

Matching colors or colors that are close neighbors will look calmer together.

COOL COLORS

WARM COLORS

"Warm" colors (oranges, reds) look good in winter and "cool" colors (greens, blues) look nice and bright in summer.

USING COLOR IN CLOTHES

Dark colors tend to fade into the background, and light or bright colors will stand out and draw attention to that part of the garment.

Notice how the all-black dress compares with this color-blocked dress—the parts of the dress with bright and light colors really jump out at you, don't they?

The burgundy accessories and pink belt on these two outfits are accent colors.

If you're not sure about the best place for a color, try using it as an "accent" in jewelry, a scarf, or a belt. Color can really change an outfit!

Tones or different shades of the same color worn together can also look great.

49

Color palettes

A color palette is a group of colors that fashion designers choose to use for lots of different pieces. These colors help all the different pieces look part of one family—the collection.

All these colors have been taken from this picture of an ornate Moroccan doorway.

You can choose to have many different colors in your palette...

...or you can use shades of just a few colors.

You can create a color palette from a mood board.

To make a color palette, look back at pages 48 and 49 and then think about:

- What season it is—do you want to use warm or cool colors?

- Harmony—all the colors should look good next to each other, unless you want things to clash.

- Accents—it's a good idea to have an "accent" color. This is a color that is brighter, lighter, or in contrast to the other colors for use in prints, trims (such as tape/ribbon/buttons), linings, or even stitching.

DESIGNER'S TIP

Using images from your mood boards, create a color palette in the sketchbook pages using what you've learned about how color works. Aim to use no more than six colors in each group.

Patterns

Many fashion designers use pattern to create a "signature" style. This is what makes their clothes look recognizable and distinct from those of other designers. Pattern can be used in many ways to create different looks.

ELEY KISHIMOTO

is known as *"the patron saint of print!"*

DESIGNER'S BRIEF

Design a small and a large pattern using the ideas on your mood boards. Pick out just one image or shape from your mood boards to make the pattern.

DIANE VON FÜRSTENBERG

mixes strong colors and bold patterns.

PATTERN MAGIC

You can alter the look of a garment by using different size prints and by using the print in different places.

LARGE OR SMALL?

Large prints need plenty of fabric to show them off.

HORIZONTAL OR VERTICAL?

Choosing vertical or horizontal stripes can affect how long and how wide a garment looks.

USE AS A DETAIL

A small piece of print used as a highlight will draw attention to that part of the garment.

COLOR BLOCKING

Using color and print blocks can trick the eye. Bright colors and bold prints will look bigger than anything else.

Silhouettes

The silhouette is the overall outline of the body that you want your designs to create. For example, you might want to highlight one area, such as the shoulders, or make the body shape appear straight up-and-down.

Using a pale color against black tricks the eye to make the silhouette thinner.

The tucks on the waistline draw your eye to that area.

Loose folds give an up and down silhouette.

This shape highlights the upper body.

Skintight jeans define a sleek silhouette.

Bell bottoms create a triangular shape.

A high waist gives a longer silhouette.

The full skirt and tight waist create a rounded "hourglass" shape.

DESIGNER'S BRIEF

Find three images from your mood board(s) and use them to draw a silhouette for an outfit or for a single garment.

Silhouettes in history

In fashion history, it is the silhouette that has most often changed.
Can you figure out which decades these silhouettes are from?
(The answers are at the foot of the page.)

A

Long
skirt

B

Mid-length
skirt

C

Narrow
waist

D

Short
skirt

E

Bell
bottoms

Wide
shoulders

F

G

Tight
jeans

A: 1900s B: 1910s C: 1940s D: 1960s E: 1970s F: 1980s G: 2000s

ANSWERS

Designers use silhouettes to follow the natural lines of the body or to create a totally different shape.

CHRISTIAN DIOR

was an influential French designer who created particularly feminine designs. His "New Look" collection of 1947 exaggerated the narrow waist and hourglass shape of women.

CRISTÓBAL BALENCIAGA

was a Spanish designer who often came up with silhouettes that weren't at all like the female body. He created this cape in 1963.

57

Playing with silhouettes

Another way you can create different silhouettes is to play around with existing garments and change them by using belts, safety pins, clips, and so on.

The shape of this boxy, loose-fitting top has been transformed using a safety pin.

Two big tucks at the back not only shape the waistline but also give the top a little flare at the hem when you look at it from the side.

Everyone has a plain cardigan.

Give it some instant shape with a wide belt.

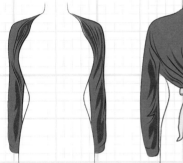

Or turn it into a shrug with tails by tying back the sides with ribbon.

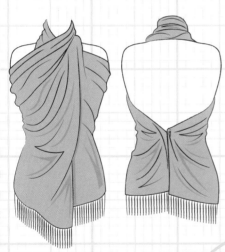

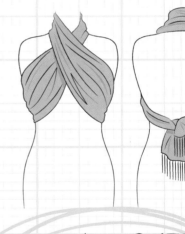

And one scarf can make so many shapes: halter top, bikini-style top, bandeau top. It can even make a skirt!

DESIGNER'S BRIEF

Change the silhouettes of some of your clothes using belts, safety pins, ribbons, or whatever else you can find! Take photographs of a friend wearing them and store them on your sketchbook pages.

Drawing

Now that you have some ideas on how you want your collection to look, think about how to draw it!

DRAWING DRAPES...

Draped styles are feminine but can be difficult to draw. Here are some tips to get you started:

The amount of shading and color you add can change the kind of drape and the type of fabric your drawing represents.

You can draw different types of drapes by changing the thickness and the shape of your lines.

Use a lighter shade on the rest of your garment.

DESIGNER'S TIP

Draw one of your own garments that drapes—a scarf or hood or a baggy top. Focus on drawing the lines and shading the drapes.

Getting the details right in your drawings can really bring your designs to life.

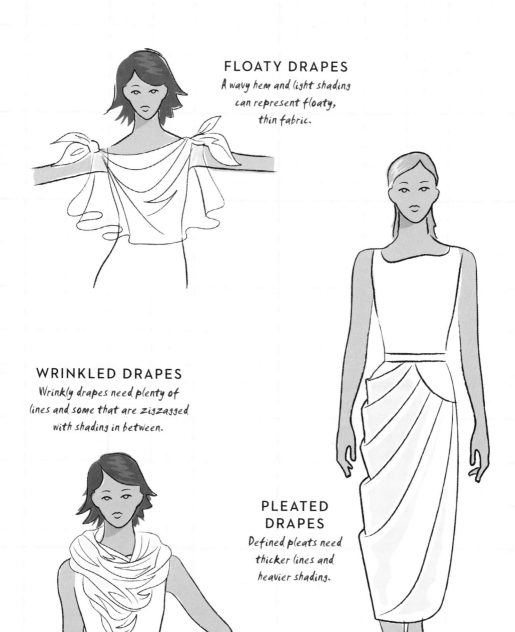

FLOATY DRAPES
A wavy hem and light shading can represent floaty, thin fabric.

WRINKLED DRAPES
Wrinkly drapes need plenty of lines and some that are zigzagged with shading in between.

PLEATED DRAPES
Defined pleats need thicker lines and heavier shading.

Drawing sleeves

All sleeves will crease and gather when they are worn, most often under the arm and at the elbow. Getting creases in the right places will help your drawings look much more lifelike. Try designing some different sleeves—don't just go for the ordinary.

Here are just a few to get you started:

When the arm is straight, wrinkles can form at the sides of the elbow, especially in close-fitting sleeves. You can draw them like this.

When the arm is bent, creases and folds are made at the inside of the elbow of the sleeve. You can draw them like this.

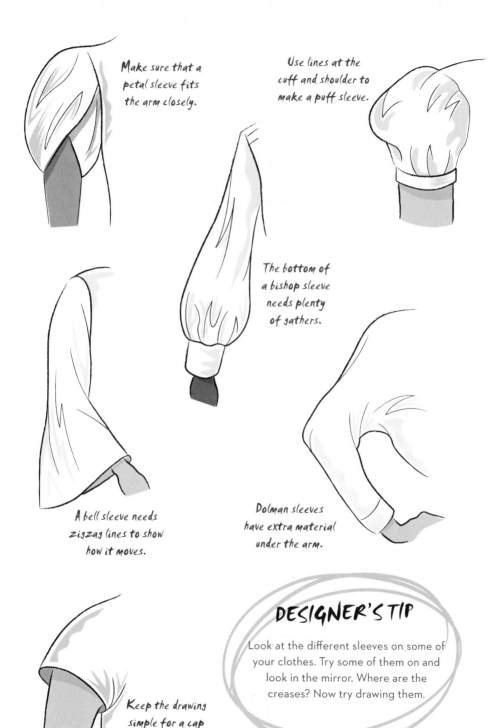

Make sure that a petal sleeve fits the arm closely.

Use lines at the cuff and shoulder to make a puff sleeve.

The bottom of a bishop sleeve needs plenty of gathers.

A bell sleeve needs zigzag lines to show how it moves.

Dolman sleeves have extra material under the arm.

Keep the drawing simple for a cap sleeve.

DESIGNER'S TIP

Look at the different sleeves on some of your clothes. Try some of them on and look in the mirror. Where are the creases? Now try drawing them.

Drawing gathers

Gathers can be used in many ways and in different places on clothes. The thickness of the fabric can completely change the look of gathers.

Gathers can be one of the most difficult details to draw. Here are some examples and tips to help your drawing:

Use a thick pen to draw the wavy outline.

Draw the basic outline of the garment lightly with pencil.

Use pens of varying thickness to add more gather lines.

DESIGNER'S TIP

Look in your closet for a piece of clothing with gathers and try drawing it.

Here are some ways of using gathers:

You could draw a full
gathered skirt...

...or a garment where
every hem is gathered.

Add gathered details, such as
collars, cuffs, and ruffles...

...or just gather some
parts, such as the
shoulders and skirt.

Drawing collars

You can make a big difference to the look of a garment by altering the collar.

You can have two collar styles on one outfit.

Sketch in the shape of the garment first, then add the collar.

There are many different styles of collars.
Here are a few examples:

A typical shirt collar has
corners that can be
rounded or sharp.

This narrow mandarin
collar stands up.

A Peter Pan collar is flat,
usually rounded, and can
be any size.

A collar and lapel
looks really smart.

A wing collar has a
defined point at
the ends.

A "pussycat" bow has long
ties that can be knotted
with the ends left long, or
tied in a fancy bow.

DESIGNER'S BRIEF

Draw the collar of one of
your shirts or tops, then try to design at
least five different collar styles for
the same garment.

Drawing flats

"Flats" are line drawings of garments that aren't drawn on a body, but look as if they were just lying on a flat surface (hence the name).

Flats are used by designers to show the people who will make the clothes exactly how they should look. Flats need to include all the details, even stitching lines, and show the back and the front of the garment. Here are some examples:

Flats don't have to be in color, but these show at a glance all the colorways (all the different color combinations that a garment will be available in) of the garments in the collection.

See how much detail is included in these flats—stitching lines, fold lines, and how they look from the back as well as the front.

Look carefully at the style of this dress and then see how the flat drawings have been created from it.

Different lines, such as swirls, can be used to indicate different fabrics and textures.

The repeated vertical lines show the folds in the skirt.

DESIGNER'S TIP

Lay out a piece of clothing on the floor or on a table and try making a flat drawing of it. Include everything—fastenings, stitching lines, seam lines, and waistbands.

Figure illustrations

Drawing people can be difficult even for the most talented artists, but being a fashion designer is all about communicating your ideas, not creating works of art!

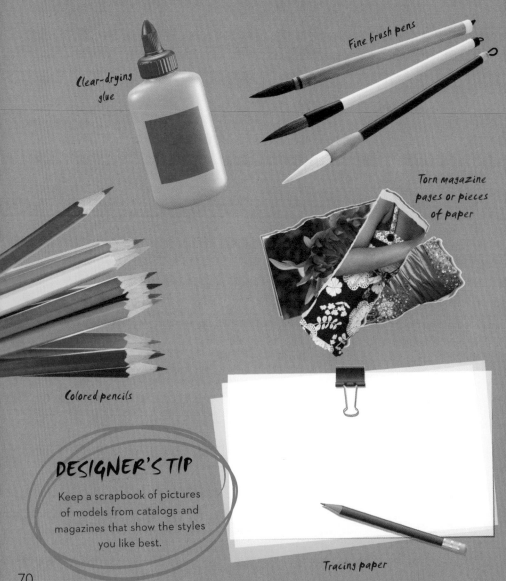

Clear-drying glue

Fine brush pens

Torn magazine pages or pieces of paper

Colored pencils

DESIGNER'S TIP

Keep a scrapbook of pictures of models from catalogs and magazines that show the styles you like best.

Tracing paper

The sketchbook pages in this section of the book include faint templates of figures onto which you can draw your designs.

With these templates, you can try out a number of styles by using different techniques for adding color and drawing outlines.

Here are some examples of "straight-up" figure illustrations done in different ways:

Sketch your outline onto the figure using a pencil.

Draw the outlines in pencil, then go over them with a fine or thick brush pen.

Color in your design using colored pencils.

Fill in your design by gluing on cut-up pieces of paper.

Sketchbook pages for your designs

Use these pages to put together a color palette and to experiment with some prints and silhouettes. At the end of this section you'll find figure templates which you can draw your designs onto.

You will then be able to start creating the designs for your collection!

DESIGNER'S TIP

Start with a color palette—
remember to use your
mood boards!

DESIGNER'S TIP

Now try designing some prints using images from your mood boards.

DESIGNER'S TIP

Practice drawing flats—raid your closet, and draw loads of different clothes! Try your best to get in all the details so that they look really lifelike.

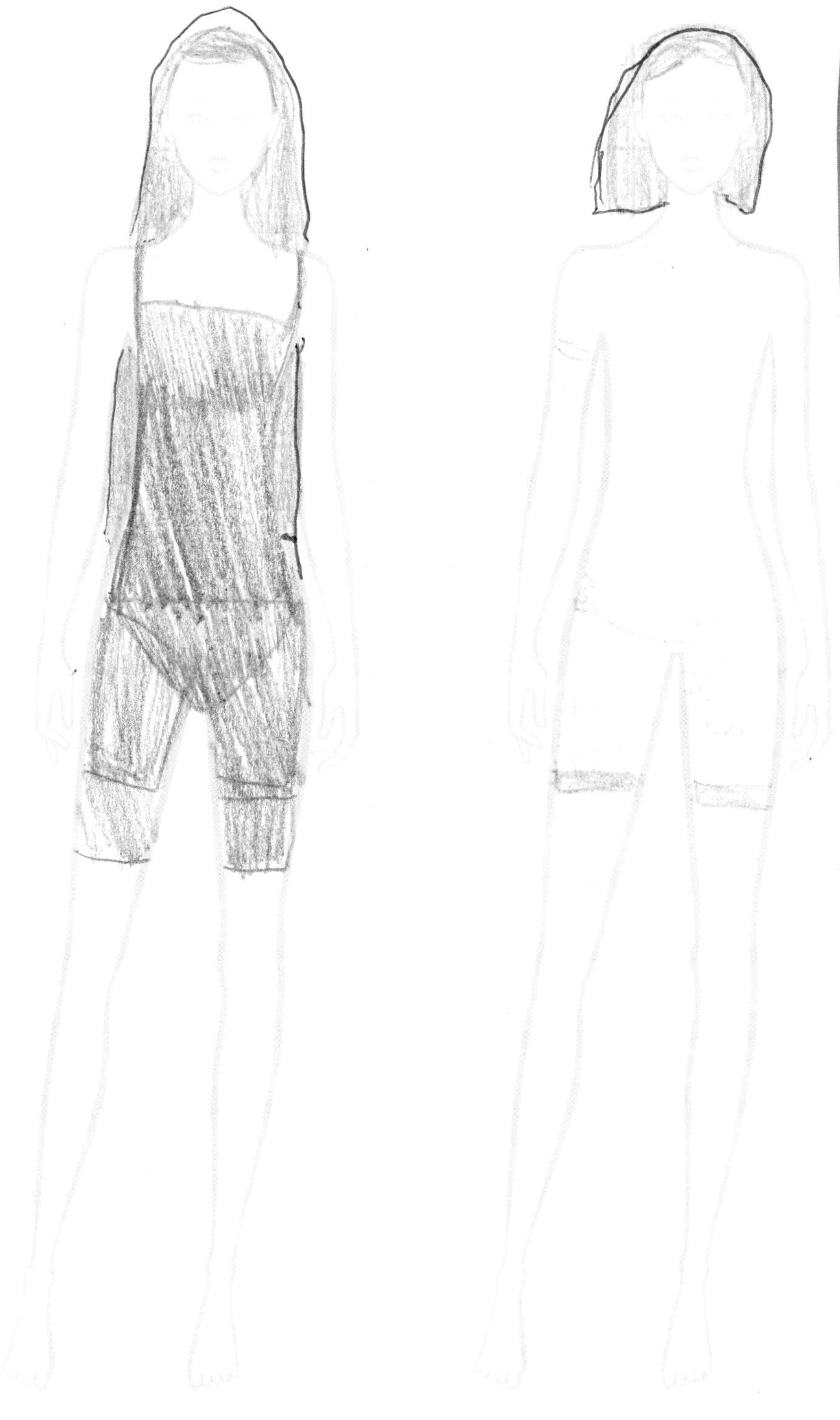

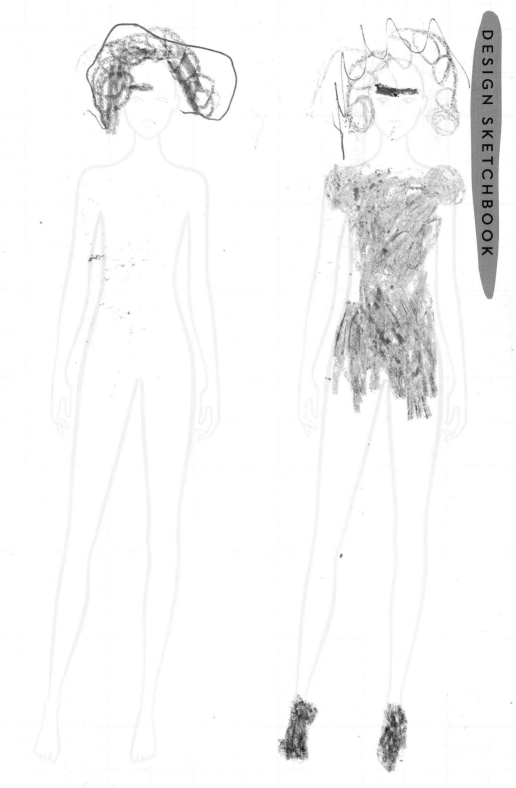

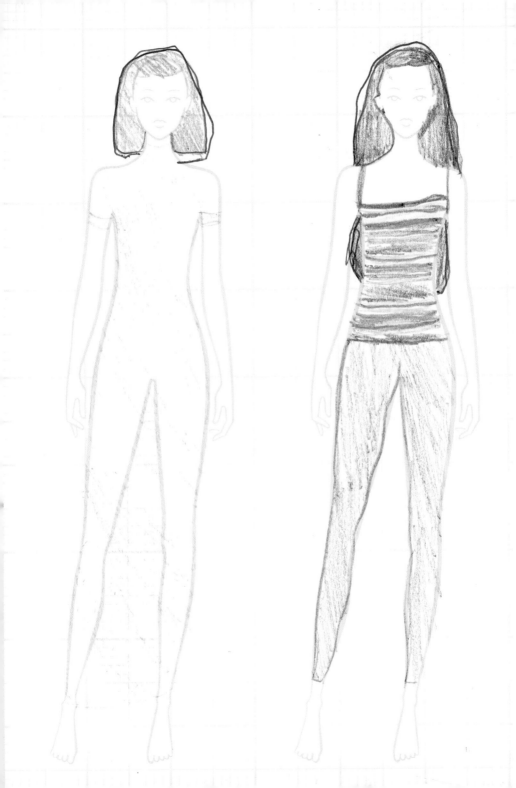

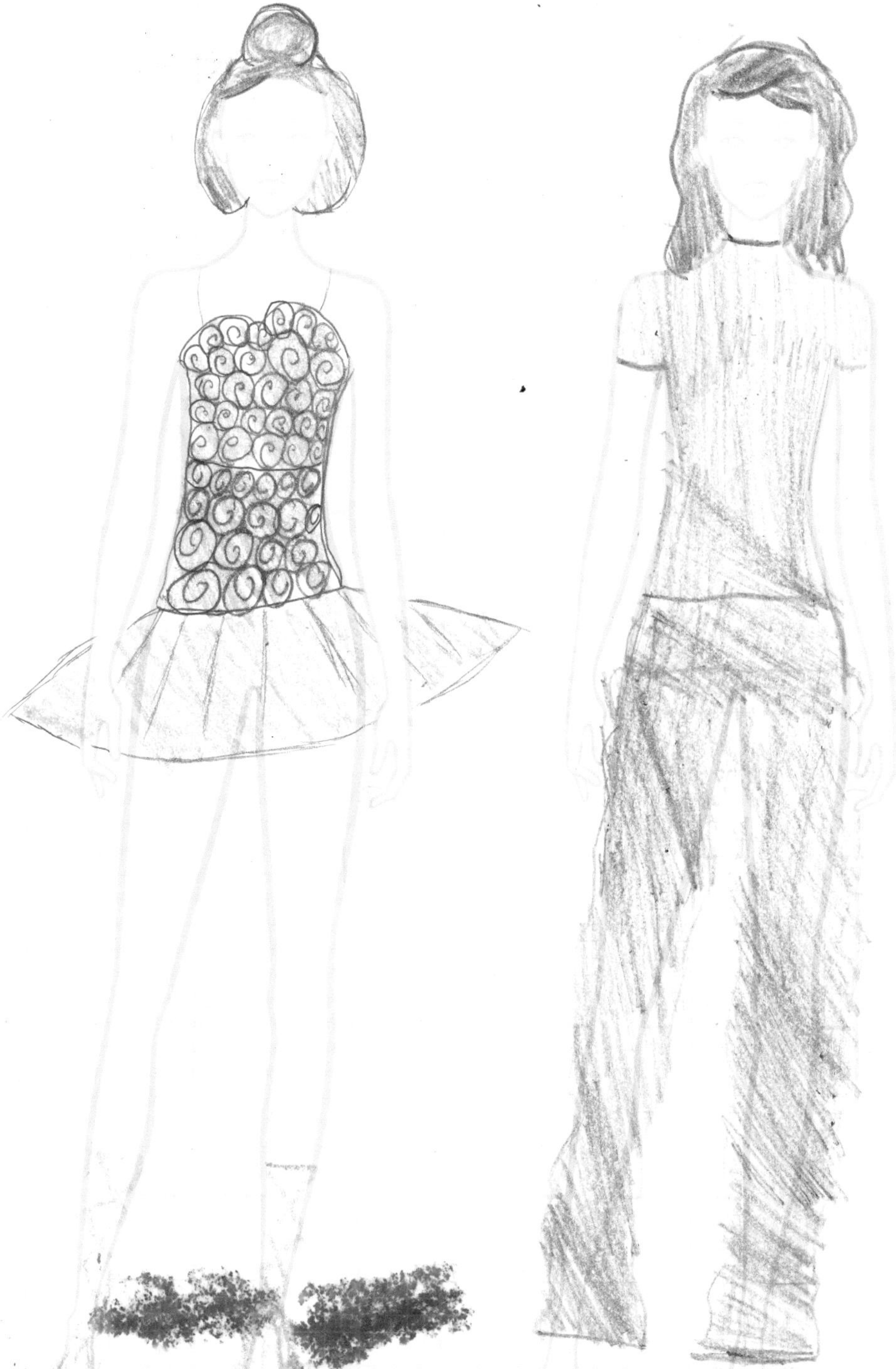

Your Collection

By now you should be bursting with
ideas for your collection! What colors,
patterns, and shapes will you use?
And will it be for yourself or for someone
else? Remember that a story or theme
should link all your ideas.

Now you can finalize your favorite
designs and style them up with accessories.
Accessories can really change the
overall look of your designs and help
you develop your theme.

Bags and shoes

You can use bags and shoes to create all kinds of styles.

These bags and shoes are tomboy, boho, party girl, and preppy. Which do you think is which? Answers at the bottom!

1

2

3

4

5

6

7

8

1 PARTY GIRL SHOES   2 PREPPY SHOES   3 BOHO SANDALS   4 TOMBOY SHOES
5 BOHO BAG   6 PREPPY BAG   7 TOMBOY BAG   8 PARTY GIRL BAG
ANSWERS

Here are some tips for drawing bags
and shoes:

It's easier if you try to draw bags from an
angle instead of straight on from the front.

1

Draw the basic shape or
outline of the bag.

2

Fill in the details and
add color.

3

1

For shoes, first draw the basic
shape of the foot and ankle
in pencil.

2

Then, sketch in the
shoe around it.

3

Add details, such
as an ankle strap
and colors.

Hats, scarves, and jewelry

These accessories make all the difference to an outfit. With the same basic clothes, you can create many different looks by using the right hats, scarves, and jewelry.

Here are some tips for drawing accessories:

EARRINGS

1

Trace over
a photograph
of your jewelry
or a picture from
the Internet.

2

Add your own
colors or change
the shape.

HATS

1

Start with a
basic shape.

2

Draw in some
details and color.

3

Add a band and
feather for a
finishing touch!

SCARVES

1

Sketch a
flowing outline.

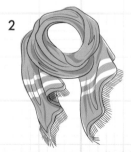

2

Add color
and details,
like fringes
or beads.

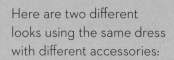

Here are two different looks using the same dress with different accessories:

Add jewelry and earrings.

Add the scarf and hat.

Choose a bag to complete your outfit.

DESIGNER'S BRIEF

Pick a garment from your designs and draw three "looks" by adding different accessories to it.

Designing your collection

Now it's time to start designing! You can use the sketchbook pages at the end of this section to help you.

First, decide who the collection is for. Is it for you or for someone else? Your best friend? Your sister? To help you decide what to include, you can create a "profile" board.

LOVES
DOING
designing jewelry

FAVORITE COLORS
red and silver

PET SHE
LOVES
cat

FAVORITE CITY
Paris

PROFILE BOARD

Your profile board should be like a mood board that reflects the personality and tastes of the person you are designing your collection for.

TOP ACCESSORY
flower hair barrette

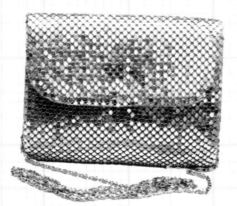

FAVORITE THEME
vintage

99

Presenting your collection

It's time to create your final collection presentation! Follow this guide to put it together:

- Look back at your drawings and decide which ones worked the best.
- Try to choose designs for 10 garments: five tops, two pants/skirts, two dresses, and one coat or jacket.
- All the garments in your collection should mix and match with each other in silhouette and color.
- Keep your mood boards and profile board in mind!

This example of what your collection could look like draws inspiration from the Paris mood board on pages 12-13, and the profile board from pages 98-99.

DESIGNER'S TIP

Look in some of your favorite store windows and see how outfits are styled and accessorized. Photograph the ones you like and use them as inspiration to help you create your collection.

COLLECTION NAME: *Party in Paris!*

Add a color palette with the colors your profile person likes. We've used a "sea" blue.

Include flat, colored drawings of your designs.

Don't forget to include accessories to complete the "look."

Look at the drawings you made in your sketchbook and use the ones you like.

Use themes from your mood boards such as polka-dot fabric and the Eiffel Tower.

101

Sketchbook pages for your collection

This section of sketchbook pages includes figure templates for you to draw your collection on to. There are also some blank pages next to them—use these to include flat drawings, accessories, and maybe even fabric swatches.

Bring your collection to life!

3 peice parts

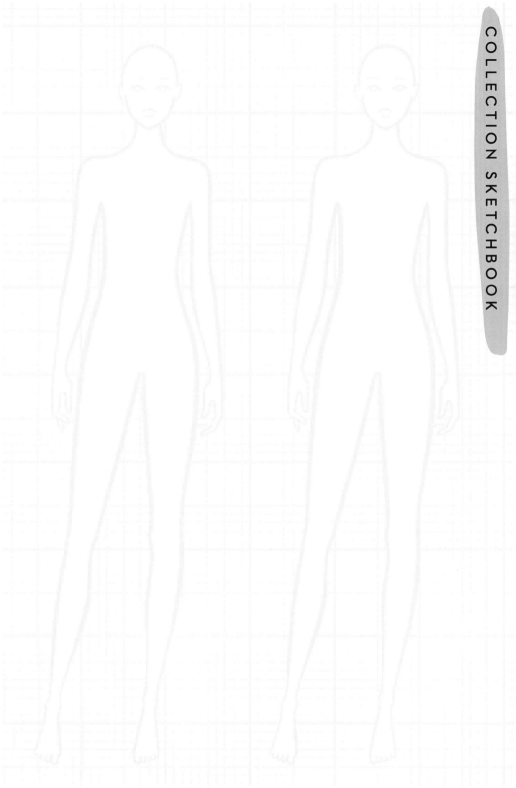

DESIGNER'S TIP

Color, color, color! Don't
leave it black and white...

DESIGNER'S TIP

Try to use some of your own
patterns and prints in
your designs.

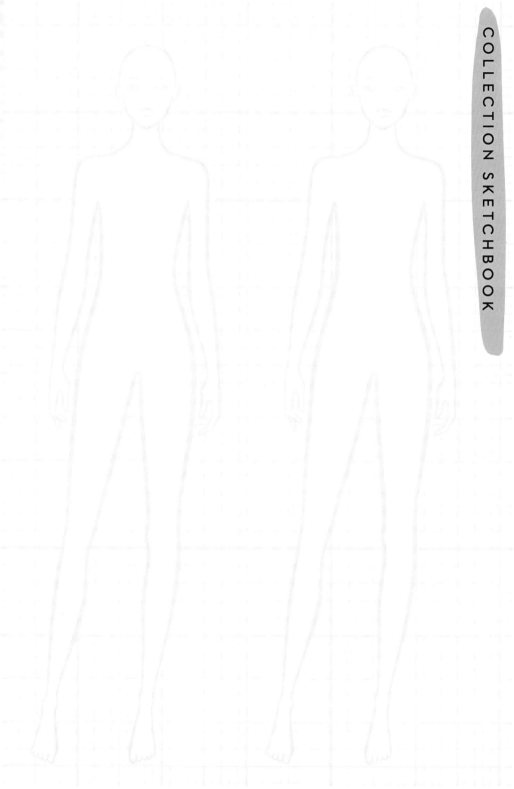

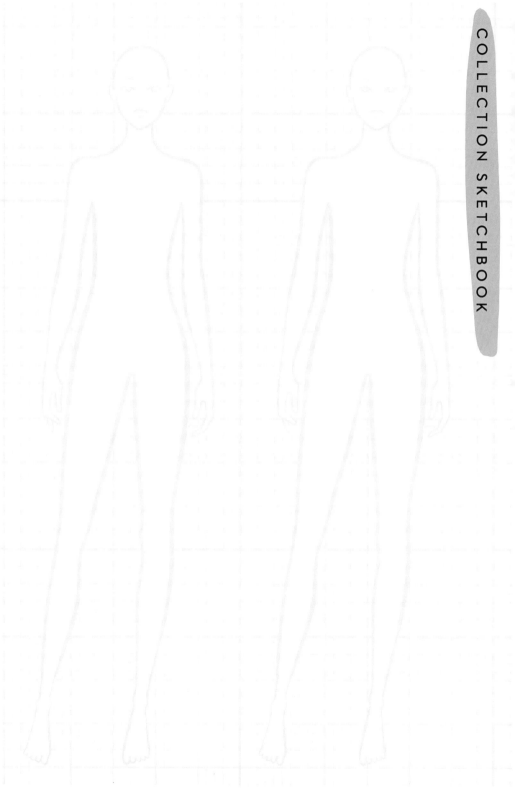

DESIGNER'S TIP

Make sure you include the
details of your designs—fabric,
buttons, and stitching.

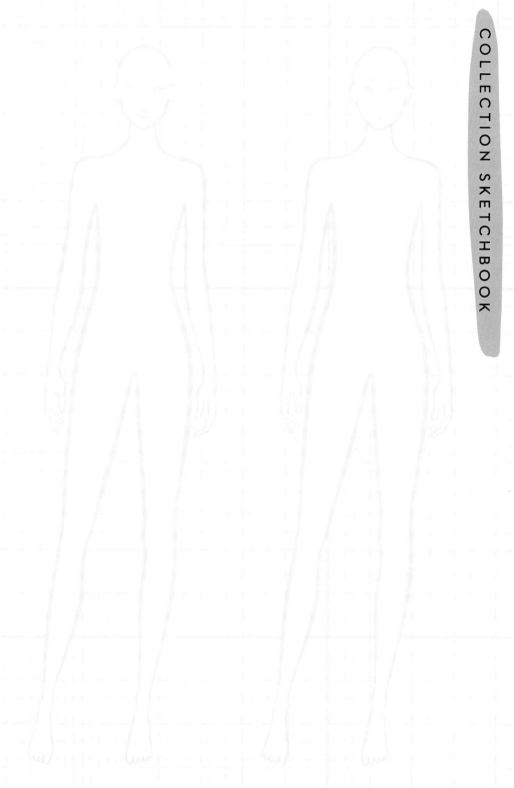

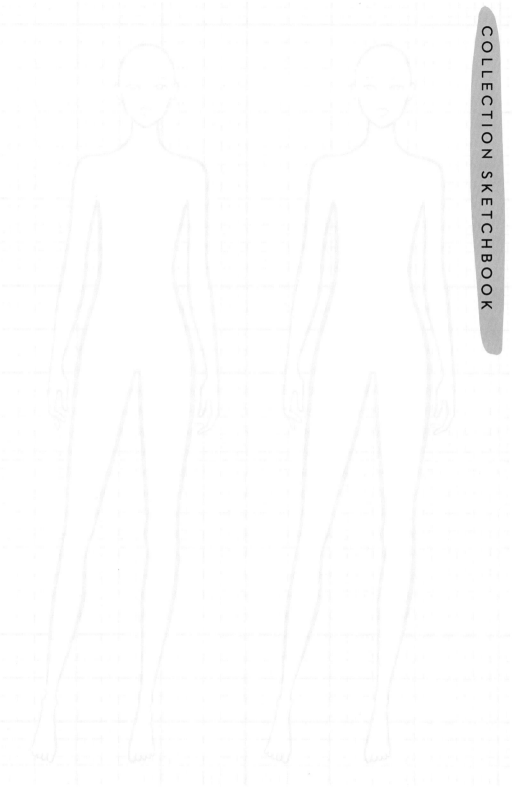

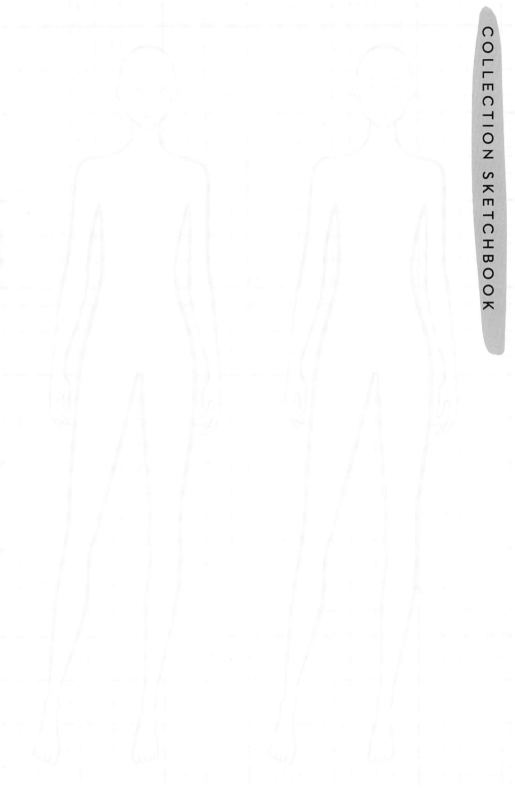

DESIGNER'S BRIEF

Look back through your collection
and choose the pieces you think work
best—scan these and then create
your own digital lookbook!

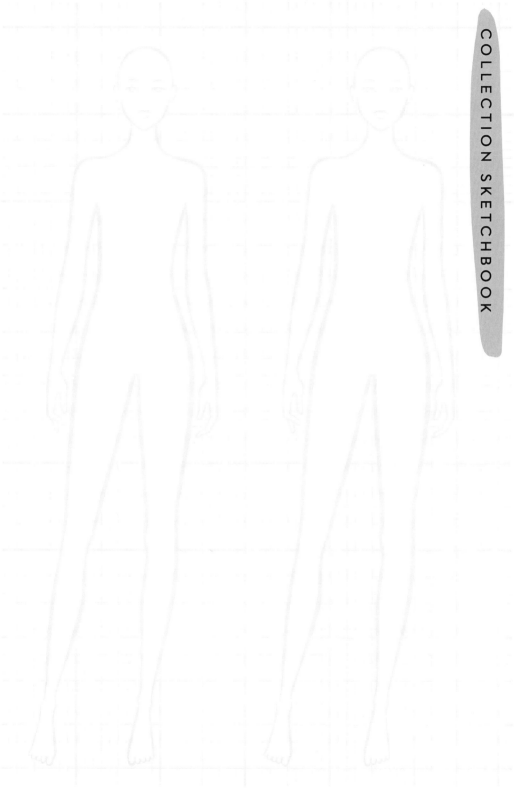

Next steps

Now that you've started, keep going!
Here are a few ideas for what to do next:

LEARN MORE

Maybe you eventually want to study fashion design. Until then, start
exploring fashion magazines, books, and blogs about fashion. Find out if
there is an after-school or weekend fashion design course for teens in your
area. Plan some mini projects—design a mini beach collection for your
vacation, design a weekend wardrobe...you get the idea. Just do it!

START SEWING—TURN YOUR IDEAS INTO REALITY!

How about actually making some of your designs?! All you need is some fabric, thread, and a sewing machine. Is there someone in your family who could teach you how to sew or a sewing club at school? If not, there are many classes and some excellent sewing books for beginners, complete with projects for people just like you.

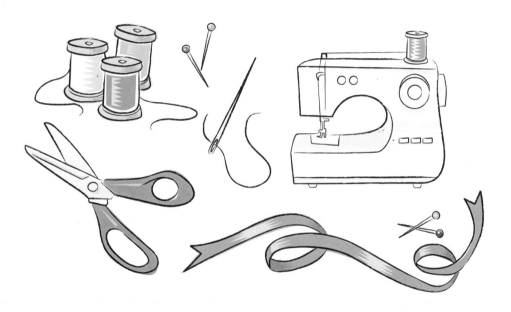

EXPLORE ART, DESIGN, AND FASHION DESIGNERS. . .

Start visiting exhibitions on art and design in general. Take a look at fashion designers' work on their websites and the many websites that report on all the fashion shows.

ACKNOWLEDGMENTS

My dad for giving me my first sewing machine; my first textiles teacher at school, Jenny Cross, who channeled my enthusiasm; Mary Braddock, an amazing pattern cutting teacher; and now my own students, who are a constant source of inspiration and a great sounding board for my ideas!

Wendy Ward

PICTURE CREDITS